writing**job**
descriptions

ALAN FOWLER

Alan Fowler has worked widely in both the private and public sectors, with personnel appointments in four industries and two local authorities. He is now a freelance consultant, a director of Personnel Publications Ltd, and a member of the editorial board of *People Management*, the bimonthly journal of the IPD. He writes widely on personnel issues, with regular articles in *People Management* and the *Local Government Chronicle*. His books include *The Disciplinary Interview* (1996) and *Negotiating, Persuading and Influencing* (1995), both in the Management Shapers series; *Negotiation: Skills and strategies* (2nd edn 1996); *Get More – and More Results – from Your People* (1998); *Get More – and More Value – from Your People* (1998); *Managing Redundancy* (1999); and *Induction* (1999). All are published by the IPD.

Management Shapers is a comprehensive series covering all the crucial management skill areas. Each book includes the key issues, helpful starting points and practical advice in a concise and lively style. Together, they form an accessible library reflecting current best practice – ideal for study or quick reference.

The Institute of Personnel and Development is the leading publisher of books and reports for personnel and training professionals, students, and all those concerned with the effective management and development of people at work. For full details of all our titles, please contact the Publishing Department:

tel. 020-8263 3387
fax 020-8263 3850
e-mail publish@ipd.co.uk

The catalogue of all IPD titles can be viewed on the IPD website:
http://www.ipd.co.uk/publications

writing job descriptions

ALAN FOWLER

INSTITUTE OF PERSONNEL AND DEVELOPMENT

First published in the *Training Extras* series in 1997
First published in the *Management Shapers* series in 2000

Design by Curve
Typesetting by Paperweight
Printed in Great Britain by
The Guernsey Press, Channel Islands

British Library Cataloguing in Publication Data
A catalogue record for this book is available from the
British Library

ISBN
0-85292-866-1

**INSTITUTE OF PERSONNEL
AND DEVELOPMENT**

IPD House, Camp Road, London SW19 4UX
Tel.: 020-8971 9000   Fax: 020-8263 3333
Registered office as above. Registered Charity No. 1038333.
A company limited by guarantee. Registered in England No. 2931892.

contents

Other titles in the series:

what job descriptions are used for

Introduction

Job descriptions are sometimes thought of as little more than bureaucratic documents that may have to be issued to newly appointed staff, but that are subsequently put in desk-drawers and largely forgotten. Jobs then change over time as duties are added or disappear, but the original job descriptions are not updated until, perhaps, an employee leaves and recruitment begins for a replacement.

Some managers and management writers go further and suggest there is no need for job descriptions at all. They argue that any formal definition of a job inhibits flexibility by restricting its activities to what has been written into the description, and creates too rigid a distinction between the job and the person in it. A job, they argue, should be built up around the capabilities of the employee, not treated as a package of duties to which the employee has to adapt.

Of course, if little importance is placed on job descriptions they will soon fall into disuse; and if they are written and used too restrictively they can make it difficult to achieve necessary changes in job content. But these objections apply only when job descriptions are not being used constructively to contribute to the effectiveness of several important people-management functions. Clearly written job descriptions, tailored to the specific purposes for which they are to be used, are an important element in three personnel processes, in each of which they serve several objectives. These processes are:

● selection, recruitment and induction

■ performance management and appraisal

▲ job evaluation (job-sizing).

Job descriptions may also be of some help in identifying (or at least suggesting) possible training needs, although this calls for a much more detailed analysis of the demands of the job in terms of knowledge and skills than job descriptions are designed to produce.

Job descriptions for recruitment, selection and induction

In the recruitment and selection process, job descriptions have three main uses:

● to provide information needed in determining the selection criteria

 ■ to inform applicants about the nature of the job

 ▲ to ensure that newly appointed staff understand the primary purpose and principal functions of the job and its place in the structure of the organisation.

Two documents form the basis for effective recruitment and selection: the job description, which sets out the purpose and functions of the job; and the person specification, which defines the selection criteria – the knowledge, experience, and other qualities to look for when selecting the person to be offered the job. It is important that these selection criteria are realistic in relation to the nature and demands of the job, setting selection standards that are neither unnecessarily high nor too low for the nature of the work.

The job description can be used as the starting-point for this analysis, because without a clear understanding of what the job involves it is impossible to ensure the validity of the selection criteria. To give just one example, if it is clear from the job description that the job involves significant face-to-face contact and discussion with customers, one of the selection criteria will need to be a good standard of verbal communication skills. Each of the main elements in the job description can be taken in turn and the question asked: 'What specific knowledge or skill is needed, and to what standard, to perform this part of the job satisfactorily?' There may well be certain aspects of the selection criteria, such as some personality factors, that are not evident from the job description and require broader consideration, but the job description should form the basis for the person specification – the two documents are complementary.

Most potential candidates are initially attracted by job advertisements, whether in the general media, trade press, or on the Internet; or by brief details supplied by a recruitment agency. Job advertisements should, of course, be accurate and provide at least basic details of the work, the organisation, the job's location, and the salary level. But advertisements need to attract attention, so their text must be brief. They rarely include sufficient detail to enable applicants to make a fully informed decision as to whether or not the job is really what they wish to aim for. This is where job descriptions come into the process.

For anything other than simple or basic jobs it is a sound selection practice to include an invitation in the job description to apply for further particulars. The information pack that is then sent out should include the job description, together with more general information about the organisation and the principal terms and conditions of employment. An element of self-selection will then occur. Some applicants will decide on the basis of the description that the job is not what they assumed from the advertisement, and that they do not wish to take their application further. Although part of the drop-out is caused by people who send for the job details simply out of curiosity, the self-selection that occurs at this stage saves time and money that could otherwise be spent reading CVs and even interviewing candidates who might well pull out later.

It is important that the job descriptions used at this stage are clearly written and well presented. Poor-quality photocopies or descriptions full of organisational jargon are likely to generate an adverse reaction – particularly if this contrasts with accompanying and well-designed publicity material about the organisation. At the same time, it is important that the job description is precisely the same as that which will form part of the induction material for the successful candidate. It would create a very bad impression on a new employee if the description issued on starting work differed from the one sent out as part of the selection process.

The main use of the job description in induction is to ensure that the new employee has a clear, definitive statement about the principal purpose of the job, its main elements, and its reporting relationships. It provides a basic outline of the job to which the more detailed information and instruction often needed by new employees can be related, and prevents this detail from distorting the job's essential objectives and priorities. It is not a 'how to do it' document. Training and guidance about the systems and procedures involved in the work need to be given by other means, including the issue of procedure manuals, formal training, and supervisory coaching. The job description should provide answers to the questions:

- What is the job there for?
- What does it contribute to the organisation's aims and activities?
- How and where does it fit into the organisation's scheme of things?

● What are the job's main duties, responsibilities, or accountabilities?

However, the job description is neither a substitute nor a vehicle for detailed guidance or instructions about how to undertake the job's various tasks. This is a matter for procedure manuals and for initial training and supervisory guidance. The job description should paint a broad picture of the job as a whole. After studying a well-written job description, the new employee should have a clear picture of why the job is there and what it is required to produce – even if many details about actual working practices may take a long time to learn.

The next chapter considers the drafting of job descriptions and two examples – one for a simple and one for a more complex job – are given in the Appendix.

Job descriptions for performance management and appraisal

Effective appraisal systems are concerned both with achieving performance improvements and with employees' personal development. Targets or objectives that are set and assessed within the appraisal system may consequently be both task-focused (relating directly to the job) and employee-focused (relating to training and learning). There is a parallel here with the job description and the person specification – the former dealing with the purpose and nature of the job, the latter with the qualities needed for satisfactory performance.

In practice, the person specification is not used directly in appraisals, although the principle of identifying the knowledge and skills the work requires, particularly as changes occur in the job, is essential to the effectiveness of the whole appraisal process.

The job description has a much more direct part to play. Appraisal is a two-way process between the employee and his or her manager, in which a common understanding of the job is essential if agreed conclusions are to be reached about standards of performance and targets for achievement. Differences of view about the primary purpose of the job or about the nature of its accountability are sources of serious potential conflict. A mutually agreed job description that is updated as the work and objectives change can therefore form the basis for a constructive appraisal discussion about both past performance and future objectives.

In preparing for an appraisal, the appraiser and appraisee can each refer to the most recent version of the job description and check whether they consider it is still accurate. If either feels that circumstances since the last appraisal require the description to be amended, the suggested changes can be noted for discussion as the first item at the appraisal. After agreeing any revisions, the appraisal can move on to consider performance against previously specified targets. Finally, the job description (revised, if necessary) can be used as a check-list for considering performance in the job as a whole. Each element in the description can be taken in turn and such questions as the following asked:

- How well is this part of the job being performed?

- Are there any particular difficulties that need to be addressed?

- How might performance in this part of the job be improved; and should we agree any new objectives or targets?

- Are there things that the manager might do to provide better support for this element?

- Can this part of the job be developed to use more fully the skill and ability that the employee has demonstrated in its performance?

The benefit of using the job description in this way is it ensures that a rounded and comprehensive view is taken of the job and the employee's performance as a whole, avoiding undue concentration simply on a few, specific work targets. This is particularly important for jobs that have a large measure of ongoing routines. Target-setting will probably concentrate on only a minority of the total volume of work activity, and often on non-routine issues. If that is what the appraisal concentrates on, the employee's performance across the major part of the job may be largely overlooked. For example, a word-processor operator may have as a target learning how to use a new graphics software package – and may have difficulty with this. But the use of this package within her weekly routine may be minimal, and on all the main parts of the job her performance may be exemplary. Using the job description as a check-list for reviewing every aspect of her work would prevent disappointment with the graphics target from distorting the overall view of how well the whole job is being done.

Job descriptions for job evaluation

Although there are many different job evaluation methods and schemes, they all depend for their validity on basing the evaluations soundly on accurate information about jobs. Job descriptions provide the primary source of this information, although their format and (to some extent) content vary with the type of job evaluation scheme being used.

Whole-job ranking is the simplest form of evaluation, in which each job is considered as a whole and placed in a ranked order with all the other jobs. For this purpose, little more is needed than the same job descriptions as are used for recruitment or appraisal – although it is important that these are checked to ensure their accuracy before being used in the evaluation process. The same 'general purpose' job descriptions can be used for the *paired comparison* type of job evaluation, in which each job is compared in turn with every other job and rated smaller, the same, or larger.

In recent years, however, there has been a significant growth in the use of various types of *analytical factor-based* job evaluation schemes – generally termed *points-rating schemes* in the UK or *point-factor-rating schemes* in the USA. One reason for their increased use is that they are the only type of job evaluation that employment tribunals accept as potentially providing evidence of bias-free reasons for differences of pay under the legislation requiring equal pay for work of equal value. In these schemes, jobs are allocated scores for a defined set of factors – such as responsibility for resources, impact, decision-making, physical working conditions, and the like. Different schemes use different factors, so the information needed in order to produce the factor scores also differs from scheme to scheme. Conventional job descriptions are helpful in a general sense but rarely provide information sufficiently specific to each factor for definitive scoring to be produced. What many schemes consequently require are job descriptions designed specifically to elicit information about the characteristics of each job in relation to each factor. The various factors can then be the headings within the job description – a very different format from job descriptions used in recruitment and appraisal, in which the jobs are broken down into their constituent duties or accountabilities.

Chapter 4 looks in more detail at the content and drafting of job descriptions used in job evaluation.

job descriptions for recruitment, selection, induction, and appraisal

The precise format of a job description varies from organisation to organisation and with the complexity of the job. But regardless of the specific format or detailed content of the job, job descriptions should always include at least the following information:

- job title
- reporting relationships
- overall purpose
- principal elements or accountabilities
- unspecified duties.

Other information that can be useful to add, but that may either be irrelevant for some jobs or supplied in some other document (such as the statutory statement of terms and conditions of employment), includes:

- salary
- location

▲ job dimensions

● contacts

● practical requirements

● statement of contractual status.

Job title

When a vacancy occurs, it is always worthwhile reviewing the job and, if necessary, revising the existing description before beginning recruitment. Changes may have occurred since it was last looked at, or the vacancy itself may provide an opportunity to introduce change. One element worth considering is the job title. There are trends or fashions in job-titling, and the continued use of an outmoded title may inhibit applications. It is sometimes argued that titles are of very little importance – that what matters is the job's content, status, and salary. From a logical viewpoint, this may be true, but many people place more importance on their job titles than they may openly admit to; potential applicants in particular are influenced by the impression of style and status that they can project. For example, a title such as 'assistant senior financial services officer' has the ring of a bureaucratic organisation and a job of uncertain status embedded within a complex management structure.

Here are some pointers to more effective job-titling:

- Use words that are as descriptive of the job as possible – eg 'engineer', 'buyer' – rather than 'technical services officer' or 'procurement executive'.

- If possible, avoid the word 'officer' and substitute such terms as 'manager', 'adviser', 'director', or 'head of...' (eg 'head of personnel' rather than 'chief personnel officer'). 'Officer' has an increasingly old-fashioned ring and does not make clear whether the job is managerial.

- Where practicable, avoid prefixing a title with 'assistant'. Every job has its specific function, which is rarely confined to providing assistance to a senior, so it is this function that should be highlighted. For example, 'assistant personnel manager' can be retitled 'employee relations adviser' if employee relations is the core function of the job.

- Be aware of the contractual implications of the job title (see Chapter 3). In brief, changes in the job must, unless otherwise agreed by the employee, be generally consistent with the broad type of work indicated by the job title.

Reporting relationships

The two principal features about organisational relationships that should be set out in the job description are the reporting lines above and below the job. These are:

- *the job title of the manager to whom the job-holder is directly responsible.* Normally this is a single position – eg the training manager reports to the personnel director. Some jobs, however, have more than one reporting line, and in such cases it is vital that the job description explains this. For example, a divisional accountant may be a member of the division's management team but also have a functional link to the central finance department. This needs to be explained along the following lines in the job description: 'Reports executively to the divisional manager for the provision of the division's financial services; is responsible functionally to the director of finance insofar as professional standards are concerned.'

- *the job titles and numbers of staff (if any) reporting to the job-holder.* These details may also need to distinguish between staff responsible executively to the job-holder and those for whom the job-holder has only functional oversight. For example, a personnel director heading a central personnel department may have no executive control of personnel managers in each of the organisation's divisions but remains responsible for ensuring that these devolved personnel specialists are kept up to date with developments in personnel concepts and techniques. The job description may then state: 'Responsible executively for the central recruitment, training, and HR planning advisers. Responsible functionally for the professional development of the three divisional personnel advisers who are executively responsible to their respective divisional line managers.'

For managerial jobs, or jobs involving a significant amount of contact with other functions, it is also helpful to append an organisation chart, showing how the job is located within the wider organisation, together with the type and number of jobs at relevant, lower organisational levels. This need not be the chart for the entire organisation, but it does need to show the relationship of the job to those around it. For example, the chart for the personnel director in the example above might look like that below.

Organisational chart

Overall purpose

The schedule of the job's principal elements should be preceded by a statement that, in effect, answers the question 'Why does the job exist?' This sets the scene for the more detailed description of specific parts of the job and summarises what the job is there for. This statement should make clear the job's purpose (or output) as well as its principal activities (or input). For a telesales job in a technical publishing company, for example, the statement of the job's overall purpose might be:

To sell, by telephone, classified advertising space in a range of engineering and construction industry journals, in order to maximise the company's advertising revenue.

The purpose of the job is to promote the company's advertising income; the activity is selling by telephone.

In the case of an organisation's training adviser:

To provide line managers with advice on methods and sources of training to meet identified training needs, and to arrange for and monitor the effectiveness of the resultant training programmes in order to contribute to the development of a multi-skilled workforce.

The purpose of the job is to contribute to workforce development; the activities include advising, arranging, and monitoring.

In writing this type of statement about the overall purpose of the job, it is often helpful to construct a sentence that has three main components:

- a 'doing' verb or verbs, such as:
  - to plan

- ☐ to supply

- △ to develop

- ○ to design

- ○ to provide

- ○ to advise

- ☐ to negotiate

- △ to monitor.

    This highlights the principal activity or activities the job involves.

■ the object or objects of the activity, such as:

- ○ product cost data

- ☐ customer requirements

- △ maintenance contracts

- ○ human resources

- ○ strategic plans

- ○ stock levels

- ☐ production methods.

    This states what the activity is concerned with.

▲ the purpose of the activity, such as:

- ○ to keep expenditure within budgeted limits

☐   to improve production effectiveness

△   to meet customer requirements

○   to ensure optimum stock levels

○   to provide accurate and timely management information.

Both the previous examples follow this type of sentence construction.

Principal elements or accountabilities

Although some basic jobs – such as shelf-stacking in a supermarket – may consist almost wholly of one particular activity to produce one particular outcome, most have several different elements which may variously be described as duties, responsibilities, or accountabilities. The term 'accountabilities' is often used when linked to performance management systems where objectives or targets are set for each of the end results for which the job-holder is held accountable. For example, one of the accountabilities in a job description for a production engineer might be:

To design and implement new production methods that contribute to the elimination of production rejects.

(Note that this example uses the same type of sentence construction as for statements of overall purpose, ie doing verbs – 'design', 'implement'; the object of the action – 'new production methods'; and the purpose of the action – 'the elimination of production rejects'.)

Within the performance management system, one year's target might then be to reduce production rejects from, say, one in 1,000 to one in 2,000. The target may vary from year to year (and in some years no related target may be set), but the particular job element remains as a standing accountability in the job description.

It is not essential to use the term 'accountabilities' – 'principal duties' or 'responsibilities' are terms that may be more acceptable. The important point is not how these job elements are labelled but that the job description should provide a list that answers the question 'What are the principal parts of the job for which specific results or outcomes are needed if the overall purpose of the job is to be achieved?' There are four key criteria for the items in this list:

⦿ When put together they must represent all the key results areas of the job – although they may omit minor or peripheral activities.

▣ They should be concerned with the objectives and outcomes of the job more than with the detail of daily working activity. In other words, the emphasis should be on the 'what' and 'why' of the job more than on 'how' it is done.

▲ Each one should be distinct and unambiguous, and require action primarily by the job-holder.

● They should be standing features of the job that remain largely unchanged, unless the job itself is restructured.

For all but the most basic jobs, the numbers of such distinct elements normally range between four and ten. A job analysis showing significantly more than ten distinct elements may indicate the desirability of reviewing the job in order to reduce its complexity.

Here are some typical examples of brief accountability or responsibility statements:

For a receptionist:

To ensure all personal callers register and are issued with visitors' passes before they enter the main building, in order to maintain compliance with the company's security systems.

For an accountant:

To produce the monthly financial data needed for the effective monitoring and control of unit costs.

For a sales manager:

To set monthly targets for the divisional sales team which will provide the motivation and incentive to meet or exceed budgeted sales revenue.

For a personnel manager:

To advise on and contribute to systems of employee information that contribute to securing a well-informed workforce.

Unspecified duties

Although job descriptions need to be periodically reviewed and updated, it is likely that circumstances will occur from time to time in which the employee will be required to undertake some duty or type of work not mentioned in the current job description. To avoid any misunderstanding (including disputes about what work is or is not contractually appropriate) it is advisable to include a statement in the schedule of the principal elements of the job along the following lines:

such other duties as the management may from time to time reasonably require.

The contractual implications of this type of statement are explained in the next chapter.

Other matters

The job title, reporting relations, overall purpose, and principal elements of the job should form the core of any job description. Other matters that may be included are outlined below. They are:

● salary

■ location

▲ job dimensions

● contacts

● practical requirements.

Salary

The salary must be defined in the separate statement of terms and conditions of employment, which has to be given to all new employees (see the next chapter), but it may also be helpful to include salary details in the job description. This applies particularly when the organisation's pay system allocates every job to a defined grade or salary scale. It is less appropriate in more flexible systems in which salaries are negotiable and therefore cannot be defined precisely in advance of an appointment. If salary details are set out in the job description it is important that they are expressed in exactly the same terms as those in the statement of terms and conditions. There could be some confusion if the job description describes the salary as 'c. £18,000' whereas the statement quotes 'Scale B: £16,500 to £19,500'. The full details – not approximations – should always be given, and if scales of grade designations are used, their salary values should always be quoted: to state that the salary for a job is 'Management Grade PO3' may mean something within the organisation but is meaningless to external applicants.

Location

As with salary, the separate written statement of terms and conditions must include details of the place (or places) of work, so it is not essential to provide this information in the job description. However, it may help to give a full picture of the job in a single document if its description does state where the job is based. These details must be the same as in the separate written statement and their wording needs to be very carefully drafted, particularly if mobility is to be a contractual condition of employment. Because of the contractual implications, this aspect of the job description is examined in more detail in the next chapter.

Job dimensions

This element may not apply to many jobs, particularly of the more basic kinds, but can usefully be included in descriptions of complex managerial jobs. In these cases, it is helpful for applicants to be given some indication of the scale of the relevant activities and responsibilities. Typical details to include are:

- the size of the job-holder's budget

- the numbers of subordinate staff

- the financial turnover of the function for which the job-holder is responsible

- information about the nature and value of any plant, equipment or property for which the job-holder is responsible.

It is not necessary to set this type of information out in any great detail, as this example for a marketing manager shows:

Job dimensions:

-  advertising and promotions budget: £2.5 million

- sales revenue: £120 million

- ▲ marketing department staff: 11.

Brief details of this kind provide an immediate indication of the overall size or 'weight' of the job, which is all that is necessary in the job description. More information may be needed for job evaluation purposes; this is explained in Chapter 4.

Contacts

Similar considerations apply to the provision of details about the job-holder's working contacts. There is no point in stating the obvious – that the job involves contact with its senior manager and colleagues within its department or unit. But if a significant feature of the work is extensive and important contact with others – such as suppliers, government departments, overseas agents, trade associations, or trade unions – it is advisable to include brief details in the job description. An example, for an economic development adviser in a local authority, might run like this:

The job involves establishing constructive contacts with local and national businesses and business organisations, the regional government office, the public utilities, and a range of European

Union offices concerned with the promotion and funding of regional economic development projects.

Practical requirements

If significant features of the job include such requirements as extensive travel, working unusual hours, and representing the organisation at public meetings or in trade or employers' associations it is as well to include a note of these in the job description. Such requirements may not make up part of the more formal contract documentation (see the next chapter), but applicants and those offered a job need to have a good all-round picture of what it entails. For example, the need frequently to be away from home overnight on extensive client visits may be impossible for some applicants to consider, whereas others may be attracted by the opportunity for foreign travel or the higher profile that attendance at meetings of an employers' association can offer. An example for a training manager might look like this:

The job involves frequent travel to the company's six subsidiaries, located in Cardiff, Exeter, Leeds, Manchester, Belfast and Glasgow, with visits of up to five days' duration to run in-house training programmes. The training manager also represents the company at the industry's annual European training conference in Brussels.

The language of job descriptions

Job descriptions used primarily for recruitment and induction purposes should be written using terminology that will be readily understood by job applicants and new employees who have little or no prior knowledge of the way the organisation conventionally describes its processes or structure. For example, in labelling parts of their organisational structures, companies use the terms 'department' and 'division' in different ways. In some organisations, departments form the major structural units and are subdivided into divisions. In others, the two words are used in the reverse sense, with divisions the largest units, subdivided into departments. Thus a job may have the title 'divisional buyer'. Is the divisional buyer's job part of a larger purchasing department, or is it to head a purchasing function that may have several subsidiary buying departments or units? The job description should provide sufficient information to enable a job applicant to recognise the job's organisational status.

The use of jargon and abbreviations – whether in-house or of wider currency – should also be avoided. Some terms may be used so widely within the organisation or industry that it is easy to forget that applicants from other sectors may never have heard of them. For example, applicants might well be puzzled by the following (found in the job description for a health service accountant):

Ensures that payroll services from the in-house business unit are delivered in accordance with the relevant SLA.

Even if the term 'in-house business unit' is understood (and this is questionable), the abbreviation 'SLA' will certainly puzzle accountants in the private sector who have had no cause to learn about the widespread use of Service-Level Agreements in the public sector. A more intelligible entry in the job description would run:

Arranges for payroll services to be provided by the separately managed payroll unit in accordance with a service-level agreement (SLA) which specifies the quality and cost standards of the required service; and monitors the payroll unit's performance to ensure these standards are maintained.

This defines the activity more clearly, while also introducing and explaining the use of SLA terminology.

Thought should also be given to matching the wording of the job description to the type of job concerned. If the aim of the job description is to help the new employee understand the main purpose and key features of the job, the wording needs to be readily understood by those who are likely to apply. There is a tendency for all the job descriptions within an organisation to be written in the same style – the one used by managers and personnel specialists when describing work within managerial or personnel circles. This is not a problem for jobs of this type, but it is inappropriate for many other kinds of work for which simpler phraseology is far more suitable. It may, for example, be accurate to describe one element of an office cleaner's job as:

To contribute to the maintenance of a satisfactory work environment by the thorough and expeditious collection, removal, and proper disposal of all waste material.

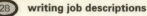

But this type of inflated language – more appropriate to the specification in a cleaning contract than to a job description – is not likely to get the right message across to the average office cleaner. A more suitable statement would be:

To help make the office a pleasant place to work in by quickly collecting and taking away waste paper and other rubbish and placing it in the correct waste bins.

Another fault to avoid is ambiguity about what the job-holder will be accountable for. A job description might include, as one element, a short statement such as:

Responsible for the unit's budget.

Does this mean the job-holder has to produce the budget, or is accountable for ensuring the unit operates within its budget, or both? Oversimplified statements about responsibilities often fail to make clear what outcomes the job-holder is expected to produce – so more explicit wording in this last example might be:

Controls the unit's expenditure to ensure this does not exceed annual budgetary provisions.

Another example of wording that is too vague might be an entry in the job description for an office manager that states:

Responsible for safety in the office.

A clearer description of this element of the job, clarifying the job-holder's accountability, would be:

Acts as the company's safety officer, arranging the necessary inspections, maintaining relevant documentation and advising senior management of the action needed to comply with legislation and secure a safe and healthy working office environment.

(In the Appendix you will find two examples of job descriptions, the one relatively simple, the other more complex.)

legal aspects 3

The contract of employment is the legal heart of the relationship between employer and employee. In particular, it determines what work the employer can require the employee to do, and at what location(s). Because job descriptions set out much of this information, their relevance in this legal context is of considerable importance, raising such questions as: Are job descriptions part of the contract of employment? Are the terms of a job description contractually binding?

Confusion or disagreement about this may occur when an employer requires an employee to undertake some new task. The employee objects on the grounds that 'It's not in my job description, so I am not obliged to comply.' Unless the issue can be resolved through discussion (which is the most satisfactory way to proceed), the result may be either an argument by the employee that the instruction amounts to a breach of contract or a decision by the employer that the employee is refusing to comply with a reasonable instruction – potentially a fair reason for dismissal. Disputes of this kind are most likely to occur when job descriptions issued on appointment become out of date through not being periodically reviewed and updated. The absence of a general clause (as explained in Chapter 2) making it clear that duties other than those specified may be required at times can also give the false impression that there is no contractual obligation to do *anything* unspecified. For all these reasons, it is important to understand the legal position. This has two components: the requirements defined by statute; and the formal, contractual situation.

Statutory requirements

Employees sometimes think that employers are required by law to issue job descriptions, and that the absence of one is in itself either a statutory offence or a breach of contract. In fact, there is no statutory requirement to issue job descriptions, although Section 1 of the Employment Rights Act 1996 defines certain details about the job that must be issued in writing to new employees. (This Act consolidated a large number of provisions in earlier statutes, including the requirement to issue statements of employment particulars that had previously been defined in the Employment Protection (Consolidation) Act 1978, updated by the Trade Union Reform and Employment Rights Act 1993.)

The relevant statutory requirement is to issue new employees with a written statement of a defined list of terms and conditions of employment within two months of the commencement of employment. The list of terms, some of which (eg 'job title') duplicate information generally provided in job descriptions, includes the:

- 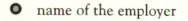 name of the employer

- job title and/or brief description of the work

- place or places of work

- date of commencement of employment

- details of any period of continuous employment

- rate of pay and its frequency of payment

- hours of work

- holiday entitlement and holiday pay

- conditions relating to incapacity absence and sick pay

- pension arrangements

- details of the job's duration (if it is not permanent)

- requirement (if any) to work outside the UK, including details of pay

- additional benefits (if any) arising from, and the duration of, such overseas work.

Whether information about pay, location, and various practical requirements are also included in a job description may be influenced by whether it is the organisation's practice to issue the statutory written statement of terms and conditions as part of the information given to job applicants. As stated above, the law requires only that this statement be issued to new employees within the first two months of employment, although it is clearly good practice to issue it at least as early as the time when an offer of employment is being made. However, it may not even then be sent to respondents to job advertisements, and in such cases the inclusion of brief details of pay, location, and practical requirements in job descriptions sent to applicants is generally to be commended.

It is important to note that the inclusion of such details in job descriptions is not a substitute for providing this information in the statutory statement of employment particulars. The statement still has to be issued – hence the advice in the previous chapter that it is necessary to ensure that details given in more than one document (ie the written statement and the job description) are identical.

Until the Trade Union Reform and Employment Rights Act 1993 (TURERA), the written statement had to include only the job title and did not have to specify the place or places of work. TURERA then put into effect the requirements of the European Directive on Written Information 1991, which stated that the place or places of work must be specified. The Directive and TURERA also permitted 'a brief description of the work for which the employee is employed' to be given as an alternative to the job title. The two key points about this provision are that:

 the brief work description is an option – it is not a requirement if the job title is specified

■ it is not a *full* job description – a brief, one-sentence summary will suffice.

In practice, most employers prefer to quote a job title rather than a brief work description, and it is difficult to think of circumstances in which it would be impossible to give a title to a job. However, if the option of a brief work description is chosen, the one-sentence description of the job's principal purpose as described in Chapter 2 should suffice. As yet, there is no case-law to indicate more clearly what the brief description must include.

The contractual situation

In determining the relevance of the statement of particulars and the job description to the contract of employment, it needs to be recognised that 'the contract' is rarely a single document – and may not even be documented. A contract comes into existence as soon as a person accepts an offer of paid employment – even if both offer and acceptance are only oral. In practice, the most important contractual document is normally the formal letter offering appointment or confirming the terms on which an oral offer has already been made and accepted, possibly supplemented by other attached documents. Alternatively, and particularly for senior managers on fixed-term or rolling contracts, a document may be issued that is formally designated as a contract – although even then it is unlikely that it would contain all the contractual terms or all the details set out in a job description.

Contracts consist of four types of terms or conditions:

● *express terms* – those specifically agreed between employer and employee, whether in writing or orally

■ *implied terms* – those so obvious they do not need to be specified, such as the requirement for the employee to comply with reasonable instructions

▲ *incorporated terms* – terms imported into individual contracts from other sources (normally from collective agreements with trade unions)

● *statutory terms* – any work requirements prescribed by law, such as those concerning the employer's and employee's duty to comply with safety regulations.

Each of these four types can influence what duties the employer has a contractual right to require from the employee, and the employee has a contractual obligation to perform.

The express terms may limit the work that can be required from the employee to a defined occupation or location. The implied terms can include ways of working that have become firmly established through custom and practice. Incorporated terms may include clauses in collective agreements that relate job definitions to particular pay scales, or define the scope of the employer's ability to transfer staff from one job or work location to another. Because the statutory written statement of terms and conditions, together with the job description, touches on many of these matters, the contractual status they are given among other employment documents may be of considerable legal importance.

Taking the written statement first, case-law has established that it is persuasive – although not conclusive – evidence that certain contractual terms have been agreed. If there is a formal contract document, its terms override those in the written statement. For example, suppose the written statement specifies a single job location, but the letter of appointment – which will almost certainly have contractual status – says the employee is required to work at any of the company's specified sites. If a dispute then arises about the company's legal right to require the employee to relocate, the terms set out in the letter of appointment will take precedence over the written statement. The only circumstances in which the written statement will be taken as conclusive evidence of contractual terms is when this has been clearly stated. So if the statement is issued with a letter that says 'The terms set out in the enclosed statement constitute your contractual entitlements' (or words to that effect), the statement is formally incorporated into the contract.

Like the written statement, job descriptions do not form a conclusive part of the contract of employment unless this is clearly stated, either in the job description or in some related document. Thus an appointment letter might enclose both the statutory written statement and a job description, and

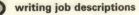

state: 'This letter, together with the enclosed documents, sets out your contractual terms and conditions.' In this case, the job description becomes part of the contract, so that any significant later change in the specified duties would need to be agreed formally by the employee. Contractual terms can be varied only by consensual agreement.

Because the incorporation of the job description in the contract can have a restrictive effect on the employer's ability to alter the job's content and duties, the recommended practice in most circumstances is to make clear that the description is not part of the contract. For the avoidance of uncertainty, this exclusion should be specific and in writing. There are two ways of doing this: a statement in a covering letter; or a footnote within the job description. The statement can be very brief:

This job description does not form part of your contract of employment.

Or:

For information only.

If this is considered too terse, a longer explanation can be given, such as:

The enclosed job description describes the principal purpose and main elements of the job. It is a guide to the nature and main duties of the job as they exist currently, but it is not intended as a wholly comprehensive or permanent schedule and is not part of the contract of employment.

The use of a statement of this kind does not mean that the job description will be wholly ignored if there is a legal dispute about the contractual right of the employer to alter the nature of the job. A court or tribunal is still likely to have some regard to the job description as providing an indication of the contractual position – but not to the extent of being bound by its precise terms. Excluding the job description from the formal contract simply helps to maintain a more flexible situation when job changes become necessary. However, to avoid legal difficulties arising from the general principles of contract law, changes must be set within the broad context of the job and not be unreasonable. Even when a general or 'catch-all' clause is included (eg 'any other duties the company may require'), it should not be assumed that this gives the employer an unfettered right to require a fundamental change in the nature of the job. For example, a catch-all clause would not enable an employer to require a secretary to take on window-cleaning duties. Any change must still, from a common-sense viewpoint, be consistent with the broad nature of the work as implied by the job title.

The job title is often common to three documents – the written statement, the letter of appointment, and the job description. Because the letter of appointment is normally taken as contractual, the job title quoted in the letter can become part of the contract, regardless of the contractual status of the written statement. This can be important if a dispute occurs about a major change of job duties imposed by the employer. In this situation, a court or tribunal may have to reach a decision about the employer's right to change the job and the employee's obligation to comply with reasonable instructions. This decision will be determined largely by the extent to which the change in job duties can be held to be consistent with a common-sense view of the nature of the work covered by the job title. Here are two examples from case-law:

- requiring a 'mechanic' to take on driving duties – this was considered outside the contract

- adding the operation of a duplicating machine to the job of a 'general duties clerk' – this was held to be within the nature of a general clerical job.

Mobility clauses

Although in most cases it is in the employer's interest to avoid the contractual specification of elements of the job description, an exception may be advisable in relation to the job's location. If the job requires the employee to work in more than one location, or if there is a possibility of a transfer to another workplace at some time, this needs to be specified in one or other of the employment documents. As noted above, there is a requirement to specify the job's location in the written statement of particulars, and this may also usefully be included in the job description. But if neither document is incorporated in the contract of employment, any such mobility clause will lack contractual force.

There are two ways of making a mobility clause part of the contract:

- by a statement that specifically brings the whole of the written statement and/or the job description, including the mobility clause, within the contract – although this may be undesirable for the reasons already discussed

- by excluding the written statement and job description from the contract, but then including the mobility requirement in the letter of appointment. In this case, the job description and/or the written statement can still include location details, but the contractual force is given by the appointment letter.

The wording of a mobility clause in whichever document it is included needs to be drafted with care. At one time it was quite common for these clauses to be completely open-ended, eg 'The company may at any time require you to transfer to another location.' More recent case-law suggests that the courts may not consider such clauses enforceable if an instruction to transfer is obviously unreasonable in relation to an employee's individual circumstances. It is consequently advisable to be as specific as possible about the locations to which transfers may become necessary, and not to impose mobility in unrealistic circumstances – such as implying that basic-grade clerical staff might be required contractually to transfer from London to, say, Glasgow. The more senior the job, the more open-ended the mobility statement can be and still be likely to be considered enforceable by the courts. Here are some examples of satisfactory mobility statements:

- *for a senior manager*: 'The job is currently based at Milton Keynes, but may be relocated to anywhere in the UK.'

- *for a middle manager*: 'Initially, the job is based at the company's London head office, but may be relocated at some stage to another establishment within the boundaries of the M25.'

- *for a salesperson*: 'The job involves extensive travel within the company's north-east region, initially operating out of Newcastle, but with the possibility of the office base being transferred to York.'

- *for a secretary*: 'The job is currently located at the company's office in Westminster but may be transferred at any time to either of the other offices in Inner London.'

Staying within the law

To comply with equal opportunity legislation and related case-law – as well as meeting the criteria of good employment practice – it is important that job descriptions include nothing that could be interpreted as discriminatory on grounds of race, ethnic origin, gender, marital status, or disability. On this and all aspects of legal implications of job descriptions, it is also important to keep up to date with developments in statute and case-law. Any future legal requirements relating, for example, to any limitations on job flexibility or working hours might require some modification to relevant elements of the examples of job descriptions in this publication. Employment legislation and its interpretation by the courts is an ever-developing and complex scene, and expert advice should be sought on any matter of concern, and also to check that nothing in this book has been overtaken by later statutes or leading cases.

General principles

The purpose of job evaluation, regardless of the type of scheme in use, is to establish internal job relativities – the relative size or value of jobs within an organisation. This can be done only if there is accurate and adequate information about the jobs to be evaluated, with some form of job description to provide the raw material for the evaluation process.

In broad terms, most job evaluation systems can be classified as either analytical or non-analytical. Analytical schemes assess jobs against a number of common factors, usually by allocating a points score for each factor, with the total of all the factor scores for each job eventually used to determine its place in list of all the jobs involved, ranked by job size. Non-analytical schemes generally consider the job as a whole and use some form of systematic whole-job comparison to produce the ranking schedule.

For non-analytical schemes, the type of job description used for recruitment, selection, and performance appraisal generally provides an adequate basis, although it may need to be supplemented by an evaluator interviewing the job-holder and his or her manager. An important point that often needs to be clarified for evaluation purposes is the scale or nature of the job's general impact on the work or objectives of the organisation, and this may not be clear from the job description.

But conventional job descriptions, even when supplemented by more information about the job's impact, are rarely adequate for analytical schemes. These schemes have become increasingly widely used in recent years. They require data specific to each factor, and this information is generally both extensive and additional to anything in conventional job descriptions. In short, analytical schemes require detailed and comprehensive job descriptions, designed specifically to match the job factors used in each particular scheme.

Job factors

Job factors are characteristics common to all the jobs involved, even though the detailed nature of the jobs varies considerably. Different schemes use different factors, so no single type of job description can be recommended. Job descriptions need to be tailored to provide the information relevant to each factor in the particular scheme in use. However, it is possible to show the general principles involved by examining the job data that might be required for a scheme based on five very commonly used factors in white-collar job evaluation. These are:

- knowledge and skill

- responsibilities
- decision-making
- complexity
- contacts.

(Other factors, drawn from a variety of schemes, are accountability, initiative, mental effort, physical working conditions, judgement, creativity, problem-solving, impact, communication, and effect of errors.)

It will be seen from this list that job factors tend to fall into two categories – those that relate to the qualities a job-holder requires to do the job effectively (in particular, knowledge and skills), and those that are features of the work itself. Conventional job descriptions do not address personal qualities, because these are more relevant in a recruitment context to the person specification. Some information about job-related factors – such as responsibility and contacts – can be drawn from the conventional job description, although this generally needs to be expanded for job evaluation purposes. What is required for each factor is information that assists the evaluators match the job against definitions of a number of factor 'levels'.

For example, the 'complexity factor' may be broken down into six levels, each with its own definition and points score – such as:

Level 1	Simple, repetitive, single task work	10 points
Level 2	A narrow range of closely related tasks or activities	20 points
Level 3	Tasks or activities with some diversity, although broadly related in subject matter	30 points
Level 4	A diverse range of tasks or activities, only some of which are related in subject matter or context	40 points
Level 5	A very diverse range of tasks or activities, many of which are unrelated in subject matter or context	50 points
Level 6	A very broad range of highly diverse and unrelated tasks or activities	60 points

Similar schedules of level descriptions will apply to all the factors in the scheme.

The job description has then to provide sufficient factual information about each factor for the evaluators (normally a panel) to allocate the job to an appropriate level. As regards complexity, for example, the job description needs to list the various tasks or activities involved in the work and indicate the extent to which they are linked by subject matter or context. Taking this factor for the second of the two jobs for which conventional job descriptions are given in the Appendix (buildings manager), a job description for evaluation purposes would need to provide such information as the:

- number of contracts being overseen at any one time

- range of types of contract (eg for redecoration, structural repairs, heating or lighting systems, ventilation equipment, grounds maintenance etc)

- variety of buildings involved, in terms of their technical characteristics (eg steel frame, prefabricated, brick or timber construction etc)

- information about management and budgetary systems

- types of subject matter dealt with in management team meetings.

The job description should provide facts about the job relative to each job factor. It should not describe the job simply by quoting the wording of what the job-holder or manager considers is the appropriate factor-level description. It is for the evaluators, not the job-holder or manager, to consider which of the level descriptions best describes the characteristics of the job, and to do so by assessing the information provided by the specially prepared job description.

Producing the job description

Job descriptions for job evaluation may be produced either by a job analyst, or more commonly by the employee and his or her manager. To ensure that all the required information is obtained and set out in a standard format, the job description usually takes the form of answers to a structured job questionnaire which explains the type of information needed for each factor. The following examples show, in condensed form, how such a questionnaire might be constructed for the five factors that this chapter is using to illustrate job evaluation principles.

Knowledge and skills

What knowledge and skills are needed for the work to be done at an acceptable level of performance? If appropriate, describe knowledge in terms of the level of actual or equivalent qualifications that are necessary (not simply desirable). List the particular skills involved in working to a satisfactory standard. How long does it take an inexperienced employee to reach an acceptable level of performance? Or how much relevant experience is necessary if you are recruiting or promoting to this job?

Responsibilities

List the outcomes (results) expected from the job and indicate what impact they make on the efficiency, effectiveness, or reputation of the unit, department, or organisation. List the specific responsibilities involved in the job for resources – people, money, plant and equipment, property – and indicate the scale in terms of numbers and financial costs or values.

Decision-making

Describe the types of decision that the job involves. Indicate the extent to which the job-holder has to use personal judgement in making these decisions, as distinct from implementing prescribed solutions. What are the constraints on decision-making – such as policies, regulations, budgets, and the need to obtain senior management approval?

Complexity

List the various activities involved in the job, together with their subject matter. Describe the extent to which these activities are either linked or diverse. Comment on the range and number of issues, topics, or cases that are 'live' at any one time.

Contacts

With which persons or organisations does the job involve significant working contact – within the organisation or externally (or both)? Show, for each, the frequency and nature of the contact and how important it is to the overall purpose or specific function of the job.

Two variants or additions to the use of fairly general questions of this kind are:

- *to use a more detailed set of questions with forced-choice answers.* For example, the questionnaire might ask for a list of contacts, with a relevant box ticked against each entry for frequency of contact:

  ○ occasional – less than monthly

☐   about once a month

△   quite frequently – more than monthly but not every week

○   frequently – about once a week

○   very frequently – several times weekly, or daily.

For the nature of contacts, the forced choice alternatives might be listed as:

○   obtaining and/or giving information

☐   obtaining and/or giving views or advice

△   lobbying and influencing

○   seeking support, endorsement, or approval

○   commercial negotiation as a client or purchaser

○   commercial negotiation as a provider.

■ *to supplement any generalised answers by asking for examples of typical cases or incidents.* For decision-making, for example, the questionnaire might include this question:

'Please give two or three examples of the most difficult decisions that have been made during the past year.'

Examples may also be helpful for such factors as complexity and contacts – and for factors in other schemes such as innovation or creativity.

To assist the evaluators gain a comprehensive understanding of the job and a 'feel' for its general characteristics, some questionnaires also include such questions as:

- What are the most difficult or challenging aspects of the job?

- What mental or physical demands does the job involve – such as long periods of concentration, disturbing noise levels, and frequent interruptions?

It is helpful also to refer to the conventional job description and ask the job-holder to annotate the schedule of principal elements with the approximate percentage of time spent on each; or to ask for a summarised list of the main activities, similarly annotated. For example, the time percentages for the job of the buildings manager (see Appendix) might look like this:

	%
Selecting contractors for tender	3
Selecting winning tenders	5
Corporate management (team meetings etc)	5
Allocating work to the unit's staff	10
Unit administration/correspondence, etc	12
Preparing or approving specifications	15
Checking/reviewing inspection reports	15
Negotiations/discussions with contractors	15
Site visits	22

The production of the job description for job evaluation begins with briefing the current job-holder about the purpose of the questionnaire. He or she then completes it and passes it to their manager for checking and, if necessary, amendment. Revisions at this stage should be agreed between the manager and job-holder, and both should sign the completed questionnaire as being accurate. Generally, it will then need to be looked at by the personnel or job evaluation specialist to check that it provides all the necessary information. Some further data or clarification may then be sought before the final version is passed to the evaluation panel for their assessment.

In summary, job descriptions for the purpose of job evaluation differ in three ways from those used for recruitment, induction, and appraisal:

- They are usually longer and more detailed.

- In particular, they include information about how the job is done – whereas conventional job descriptions are more concerned with why the job exists and what it is required to achieve.

- Their particular format is tailored to match the specific information requirements of whatever job evaluation system and job factors are being used.

key points

1

Clearly written job descriptions, tailored for the specific purposes for which they are used, can contribute to the effectiveness of:

- recruitment, selection and induction
- performance management and appraisal
- job evaluation.

They are also one source of information that can be drawn on in the identification of training needs.

2

In recruitment, selection, and induction job descriptions can:

- provide information on which to base selection criteria
- inform applicants about the nature of the job
- help new staff understand the purpose of the job and its place in the organisational structure.

3

Job descriptions should answer the questions:

- What is the job there for?
- What does it contribute to the organisation's aims and objectives?
- How does it fit into the organisation's scheme of things?
- What are its principal duties and accountabilities?

4

In performance management, job descriptions provide a check-list of the job's principal elements to which specific performance targets can be set.

5

In job evaluation, job descriptions provide the factual information on which objective assessments of the relative size or value of jobs can be made.

6

Job descriptions should always include:

Job title   Reporting relationships

Overall purpose   Principal elements

Reference to unspecified duties

7

Optional information, provided either in job descriptions or in other employment documents (or both) can include:

Salary	Location
Job dimensions	Contacts
Practical requirements	Statement of contractual status

8

Job titles should be descriptive of the general nature of the work and avoid outdated and status-biased designations.

9

Reporting relationships should show the numbers and designations of the staff for whom job-holders are responsible and the managers to whom they report.

10

Job descriptions should define the job's overall purpose – why the job is there. This is best done by a single sentence constructed of:

- a 'doing' verb to highlight the principal activity (eg to plan, supply, design, manage, produce etc)

- the object of the activity – this states what the activity is concerned with (eg cost data, customer requirements, stocks etc)

▲ the purpose of the activity (eg to keep expenditure within budget, to improve productivity).

11

The statement of overall purpose should be followed by a list of the job's principal constituent elements (duties, responsibilities, accountabilities). These can be drafted on the same principle as the statement of overall purpose.

12

The principal elements should:

● cover, when taken together, all the key results areas of the job

- be focused more on objectives or outcomes than on the detail of working activities

▲ each be a distinct function, requiring action primarily by the job-holder

◉ be standing features of the job.

13

To register the principle that duties other than those in the job description may be required at times, the job description should include a statement to this effect.

14

The language used in job descriptions should:

- avoid jargon and unexplained acronyms or abbreviations

- be matched to the type of job and be readily understandable to the employees concerned

- avoid ambiguity about responsibility and be clear about the job-holder's accountability for results and resources.

15

There is no legal requirement to issue job descriptions – their use is a matter of good employment practice.

16

There is, however, a legal requirement to issue a separate written statement of terms and conditions of employment, and this has to contain some information (job title, salary, location) that is, or may be, included in job descriptions.

17

Neither the written statement nor job description needs to form part of the contract of employment.

18

However, both documents can acquire contractual status if they are issued with a letter of appointment stating that 'This letter, together with the enclosed documents, sets out your contractual terms' (or words to that effect).

19

To maintain the ability to make reasonable changes to the job content without potential contractual difficulties, it is generally good practice to exclude the job description from the contract by the inclusion of a specific statement to that effect – eg 'This job description does not form part of your contract of employment.'

20

If there is a need to give contractual status to a mobility requirement (ie relocation), this can be done by setting out the requirement in the letter of appointment or other formal contract document, rather than relying on a non-contractual statement in the job description.

21

Conventional job descriptions may be adequate for use in non-analytical job evaluation, such as whole-job or paired comparisons, but may need to be supplemented by information about the impact of the job on the organisation's work, objectives, or reputation.

22

Conventional job descriptions are rarely adequate for use in analytical, factor-based job evaluation schemes. In these, more detailed job descriptions are needed which provide information specific to each factor (complexity, contacts, responsibilities, etc).

23

Information for each factor may best be obtained by means of a questionnaire that specifies what is required and that is completed jointly by the job-holder and the job-holder's manager.

24

This type of job description is longer and more detailed than conventional job descriptions, particularly in the provision of information about how the job is done.

further study

- References to job descriptions will be found in most publications about recruitment and selection, including *The Selection Interview* by Penny Hackett in this series (London, IPD, 1995).

- An ACAS booklet, *Employee Appraisal* (London, ACAS, 1988), refers to job descriptions in the context of the documentation needed for appraisal interviews.

- The contractual implications of job descriptions are dealt with in *Contracts of Employment* (London, IPD, 1999).

- A comprehensive explanation of the production and uses of job descriptions for job evaluation is provided in *The Job Evaluation Handbook* (Michael Armstrong and Angela Baron, London, IPD, 1995).

appendix

Examples of job descriptions (for recruitment, induction and appraisal)

Example 1: A relatively simple job

This example includes only the basic information about the job title, reporting relationships, principal purpose, and principal elements. It leaves information about salary and location to be covered by the separate statutory statement of terms and conditions of employment.

Job title
Word-processing operator

Reports to
Office supervisor

Principal purpose
To produce letters, reports and other documents from a variety of sources such as audio-tapes, hand-written drafts, and on-screen material to a standard and deadlines that meet the requirements of the authors for whom this work is produced.

Principal elements

a) To maintain a log of all work undertaken so that the office supervisor can monitor the dates, origin, and cost of each job.

b) To produce documents in the style and layout required by their authors or as instructed by the office supervisor.

c) To suggest how the layout and/or appearance of documents might be improved in cases in which the authors either seek or are willing to accept such suggestions.

d) To maintain the word-processing equipment in a clean and secure state, and to report any hardware or software problems promptly so that corrective action can be taken quickly.

e) To respect and maintain the confidentiality of the processed material and ensure that any regulations concerning security or confidentiality (such as the safeguarding of passwords) are complied with.

f) Such other duties as the management may at times reasonably require.

Note This job description is a guide to the principal, current duties of the job. It does not form part of the contract of employment.

Example 2: A more complex job

This example includes information about salary, location, dimensions, contacts, and practical requirements, in addition to the basic features shown in Example 1 above.

Job title
Buildings manager

Salary
Management grade C: £35,000 to £48,000

Reports to
Director of corporate services

Immediate subordinates
    3 × building inspectors

    1 × quantity surveyor

    1 × administrator

Organisational structure

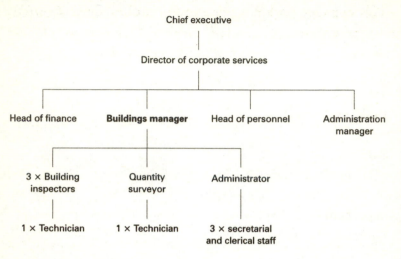

Principal purpose

To monitor the condition of the organisation's building stock and to plan, let, and oversee the necessary contracts for repairs and maintenance to ensure that buildings are maintained to required standards within relevant budgets.

Principal elements

a) To plan inspection programmes and allocate and supervise the work of the building inspectors to ensure that defects and repair and maintenance needs are identified promptly and accurately.

b) To liaise with the nominated architects in the design and construction of new building projects.

c) To prepare, cost, and plan the necessary schedules of repairs and maintenance, including preventive maintenance.

d) To prepare specifications for this work for competitive tender, select contractors for invitation to tender, and select contractors to undertake the work who provide evidence that they can meet relevant cost and quality criteria.

e) To monitor contractors to ensure that work is undertaken to specification and that claims for additional payments for contract variations are minimised.

f) To negotiate any such claims with a view to achieving final costs within – or as close as possible to – original cost estimates.

g) To monitor the performance and potential of subordinate staff and provide the direction, training, and motivation necessary to secure their optimum commitment and competence.

h) As a member of the senior management team of the directorate of corporate services, to participate in the team's discussions and decisions and so contribute to the directorate's overall effectiveness.

i) Such other duties as may from time to time be reasonably required.

Job dimensions
Staff: the 10 staff shown in the organisational structure chart above.

Budgets:

● budget for the building management unit (staff plus overheads): c. £380,000

■ maintenance and repairs budget: c. £4 million, all under the building manager's direct control.

▲ new build budget: very variable but averages c. £0.8 million per annum, generally under the control of project architects but involving advisory input from the building manager on maintenance implications of design options.

Building stock
C. 200 offices, depots, and wholesale outlets with a capital value of c. £80 million.

Contacts
The job involves close working contact with the occupiers of all the organisation's buildings to ensure their requirements and concerns are taken into consideration when remedial work is being planned. Some contact with local authority planning officers to ensure authorisation of work on a small number of buildings in conservation areas. Extensive contact with building contractors and specialists (eg environmental and structural engineers).

Location

Currently based at the Peterborough office, but the job-holder may be required to relocate to any of the organisation's offices throughout the UK.

Practical requirements

The job involves extensive travel throughout the UK with frequent overnight stays on visits to various of the organisation's facilities.

Note This job description does not form part of the contract of employment.